THE ART OF
ROCK PAINTING

by Diana Fisher

METRO BOOKS

122 Fifth Avenue
New York, NY 10011

CONTENTS

INTRODUCTION

Rock painting is a fascinating art form with a long and intriguing history. Although ancient pictographs on cave walls still communicate details about long-extinct cultures, rock painting is also a modern art form. And in this fast-paced age of technology, rock painting emerges as a wondrous anomaly. For one thing, the basic materials you need—rocks—are generally free. Also hunting for the right rocks puts you in touch with nature and engages all the senses. And painting a rock's sculpted surface is always an interesting adventure!

Every rock is a unique canvas, and each three-dimensional shape can be transformed with paint to produce brilliant results. For example, imagine a carrot-shaped rock, with the hint of organic imperfections already on the surface; all you need to make it come alive is to brush on the colors! In this book, I'll demonstrate a number of basic techniques for painting a variety of rocks, and I'll also share useful shortcuts and easy ways to create exciting special effects. Once you've begun your journey in rock painting, don't be surprised to find yourself eyeing every rock in sight for possibilities!

ASSEMBLING YOUR SUPPLIES

Everything you need to get started rock painting is in this kit, from rocks and pebbles to acrylic paints and paintbrushes. Additional materials used for the projects in this book, such as wood filler, sponges, and paper towels, are easy to purchase or may already be in your home. As you read the following pages, keep in mind that these are my suggestions—you will discover your own preferences as you develop your skills. And when you're finished painting the rocks in this kit, simply go outside to find more! If you live in a city or have no opportunity to go rock hunting, contacting a rock supplier is a wonderful alternative. Normally rock suppliers sell by the truckload, but many are willing to sell just a few rocks for a reasonable price.

Water-Smoothed Rocks The rounded contours of river rocks provide smooth surfaces that are perfect for painting. I visit local rivers and streams to find a wide variety of pleasing shapes and sizes. Water-smoothed rocks can also be found along some coastlines; in fact, just about any area near moving water may prove a good hunting ground. Remember to bring a backpack or a sturdy canvas bag to transport your treasures.

Rock Suppliers A variety of rocks, including natural rocks, can be purchased from rock suppliers. In these expansive yards, rocks are sorted according to size and type. Most of the rocks are priced by number or size, but flat flagstone is typically sold by weight. You can also find flat flagstone in a variety of colors, thicknesses, and textures. Locate a rock supplier by looking in a phone book under "Landscape Supplies."

Natural Rock Many different rocks can be found on the side of the road, from chunky to flat to round. A dry river bed is a particularly good, natural cache for rocks. I often find many interesting rocks during hikes near my home in the desert. Hiking trails, mountains, and fields are just a few of the natural sources for rocks. You may even find rocks in your own backyard that are suitable for painting. So always be on the lookout for that next perfect rock!

Acrylic Paints

You can complete all the projects in this book with the seven paints inside the kit: brilliant red, black, deep yellow, burnt umber, white, phthalo blue, and sap green. Some projects will call for you to mix colors to create new ones—you'll find brief instructions throughout the projects. For adding three-dimensional accents, buy a few squeeze bottles of acrylic fabric paint.

Brushes and Sponges

Use the round brush in this kit for general painting, drybrushing (see page 7), and other special techniques. Use the flat brush to paint large areas, base coats, and blends. Many of the projects require a liner brush for creating fine lines and details and natural sponges for applying an even, textured base coat or to create special effects. Liner brushes (angled brushes also work well) and sponges can be found at art and craft stores.

Mixing Palette and Palette Knife

The mixing palette in this kit will help you lay out and mix your acrylic paints, and you can use the palette knife to mix and apply the paint to your rocks. When you're done using the palette and knife, be sure to rinse them well with warm water.

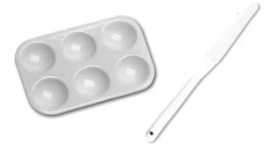

Other Supplies

Paper towels are handy for cleaning up spills and wiping brushes. Use black or white colored pencils for guidelines or transferring designs and a permanent marker for lettering. A hair dryer speeds up drying time, rubber gloves protect your hands from messy jobs, and clear acrylic spray-finish waterproofs your painted rocks. Buy wood filler for sealing holes and creating stable bases for upright projects.

GETTING STARTED

Rock painting requires no special workspace—just a flat table under good lighting. To protect the surface, cover the tabletop with newspaper and tape it into place so it won't shift. You may also want to tape down a large piece of white bond paper to create a clean surface for testing paints and brushstrokes. If your rock is not too large, place a small piece of paper underneath it; this will let you turn the rock while you work without touching any wet paint. Don't forget a container for rinsing your brushes!

Prepare Your Workspace Organize your work station before you begin painting, and place your materials within easy reach. Natural light is best, but good artificial light can also work well and let you work at night. Avoid backaches by choosing a comfortable, height-appropriate chair. And keep those paper towels handy for spills!

Prepping Your Rocks It's very important to wash your rocks well before you begin painting. If the surface dirt is not removed, it may come loose, causing your paint to chip off with it. I recommend using a plastic tub to wash the rocks so that the rocks won't scratch your sink, but you can also rinse them outside with a hose. Use a scrub brush to easily remove embedded dirt. If necessary, soak the rocks first to loosen any dirt and debris.

ROCK-BOTTOM BASICS: TECHNIQUES

Before you begin a project, it's a good idea to practice a few basic brush strokes and painting techniques. This will help you get a "feel" for your paints—how they flow and what kind of coverage you get—so that you can paint with confidence. Don't be afraid to experiment and try a variety of painting techniques. If you make a mistake and want to start over, it's no problem; remember that acrylic colors can be washed off while they're still wet or painted over after they are dry.

Drybrushing Drybrushing is an easy way to create the look of grass, fur, or anything that requires soft texture. It can also be used to build up color or to add subtle shading. First load the round brush with paint. Lay the bristles on paper and wiggle them back and forth while holding the handle vertically and pulling away slightly. The object is to wick away the wetness and to splay the bristles. Apply the paint using light, feathered strokes with the bristles splayed. When the paint dries, repeat as needed to build color and texture.

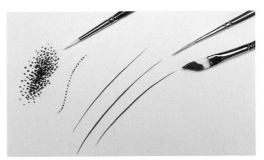

Stippling and Lining Stippling and lining are both important techniques. Stippling adds color and texture while letting the underpainting show through. To stipple, dot on the paint with the tip of the round brush. For lining, use a liner brush to make clean, thin strokes; its long bristles can hold ample paint. Angled brushes also work well for lining, especially on round surfaces. Hold the angled brush so that the chiseled edge slides lightly along the surface. Practice using long, light strokes, pulling the brush gently away from the line as you go.

Double- and Triple-Loading Double- and triple-loading your brushes will produce a variety of color blends. To double-load a brush, dip each side in a different color as shown above, or squeeze two colors side by side onto your palette, and dip your brush in both at once. To triple-load, simply add a third color. In the example above, I've inserted white between green and red to create a *gradation* effect (the appearance of one color fading into another). With this technique, one brushstroke will produce a slight blend of the colors (see "Painting Flowers" on page 15), and stroking back and forth will create a smooth, soft blend.

Wet Layering Highlighting and shading are easy to accomplish with wet layering. This technique also works beautifully for rendering rose petals. To highlight an edge, start with an application of your base color and let it dry. Then dip the round brush in clean water and wet the area just below the edge to be highlighted. Choose a color lighter than the base and highlight the dry edge, stroking it into the wet area. Dry your brush on a towel, and then use it to absorb any excess moisture. You can use this same method to shade an edge, but use a color that is darker than the base.

ZEN ROCK GARDEN: SPONGING ON COLOR

A garden is a relaxing place to work or observe nature, but a Zen rock garden can be appreciated on many levels. For centuries, these gardens have been used to cultivate creativity and instill a sense of well-being. Each stone is like a small island of tranquility. Whether it's the smoothness of the rocks; the way you arrange them in the fine, white sand; the pleasing colors; or a combination of all of these things, this Zen rock garden will provide you with many harmonious and peaceful hours of enjoyment.

Soothing Stones Sponge on beautifully blended backgrounds for your favorite Zen inspirations. (See page 11 for samples of Japanese Kanji calligraphy symbols and their meanings.)

Step One First squeeze a sponge to form a rounded surface. (Because sponging can be messy, I wear rubber gloves.) Dip the sponge in your lightest color, and dab the paint onto the exposed half of the rock until it's covered. Immediately sponge your medium color into the wet paint, leaving a portion of the top area untouched. Do not rinse the sponge between colors; rotate the sponge instead to avoid contaminating the colors. If the color is too thick, blot the sponge on paper a few times to remove the excess paint. Sponge your darkest color into the wet edge of your medium color and down as far as you can go. After the paint dries, turn the rock over and continue sponging the darkest color onto the bottom of the rock.

Step Two Set the rock on the dry side, and let the paint dry overnight. Then transfer the chosen symbols to the center of the top of the rock. (See box below.) First cut the pattern closely to the symbol to make it easier to center on the rock. Then tape the pattern lightly into place with a small piece of low-tack artist's tape (found at art and craft supply stores); transparent and masking tapes are too sticky and may pull up the sponged paint. If this does happen, don't worry—just stipple the color back on with the round brush.

TRANSFERRING A DESIGN

To transfer a design onto a rock, first reduce or enlarge the design on a copy machine to fit your rock. Color the back of the design with white pencil for dark rocks and black pencil for light rocks, so the paper acts like carbon paper. (You can also use carbon paper, but it smudges more easily.) Cut out the design and tape it down with low-tack artist's tape. To place a pattern over a very round rock, cut out triangles from the edges so the paper will conform more easily. Transfer the image by tracing over the lines with a ballpoint pen, using light to medium pressure. You can peek underneath to see if your pressure is adequately transferring the image. (Important: If your rock has been painted, allow the paint to dry thoroughly overnight; otherwise the tape may pull up the paint, or the colored pencil may smudge.)

Step Three Next paint the symbols using a liner brush. I used black paint, but you needn't restrict yourself—be creative and explore different color combinations. Try to always stroke toward the thin end of a line, lifting the brush up and away as you finish. If your strokes are skipping over the rock, dilute the paint more—being careful not to thin it too much or the paint will be runny and transparent—and stroke more slowly.

Step Four To create balance in your Zen garden, add a little yin and yang. Choose another rock and sponge the entire rock white. (Two coats may be needed if the rock is dark.) Once the paint is dry, sketch an S shape on the top with a black colored pencil. Draw the two small circles into the S curves using a circle template. Line the edges of areas to be painted black with the round brush, and then evenly fill in the black using the flat brush.

Step Five When you're done painting the rocks for your Zen garden, examine them to see if you can find any small mistakes. It's always easier to touch up errors when the paint is dry. Once you're satisfied with your results, seal the rocks with clear matte acrylic spray. (See "Clear-Coating the Finished Piece" on page 22.)

USING WOOD FILLER

When an otherwise perfect rock is marred by a hole or a crack, wood filler can correct the imperfection. Start with a clean rock. Fill in the hole with a putty knife, and then remove the excess. If desired, sand the filler after 15 minutes. Let the wood filler dry for two hours before painting.

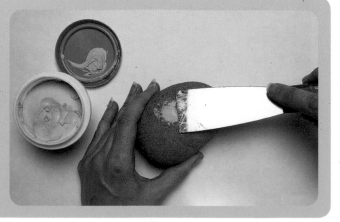

JAPANESE
CALLIGRAPHY TEMPLATES

I used "beauty," "contentment," and "harmony" in my project. Here are examples of some possibilities for you to consider:

Beauty

Peace

Harmony

Love

Prosperity

Contentment

Health

幸福

Happiness

情熱

Passion

ROCKY REFRIGERATOR MAGNETS: BRUSH PAINTING TECHNIQUES

Adorn your refrigerator with beautiful, hand-painted, 3-D flowers and insects. Use a color-ful, delicate moth to hold up your grocery list and adorable little ladybugs and beetles to anchor your children's latest school pictures. Or leave off the magnets and set your stone flowers and insects in potted plants or in the garden. Rocks are ideal for this project be-cause the small, smooth shapes you need are easily found in nature.

Fanciful Flowers and Friendly Bugs A combination of drybrushing and wet layering is used to achieve the realistic textures and color blends of these charming little flowers and insects.

Step One For refrigerator magnets, choose small rocks (I don't recommend using a rock larger than the ones shown here, which are each about two inches long). To test whether your magnet will hold the rock's weight, skip to step eight and glue on the magnet. When you're ready to begin, sketch the wings, body, head, and eyes of the ladybug (or any beetle you choose to paint) with a colored pencil.

Step Two Paint the wings red. This may require more than one coat because red is somewhat transparent, and you'll want the wings to be bright and vibrant. Allow the paint to dry between coats, or your brush will pick up the first layer of paint and mar the surface. Using your mixing palette, create orange by mixing red and yellow. Then add an orange highlight to the edges of the wings using the wet layering technique explained on page 7.

Step Three Paint the rest of the ladybug black, but leave the eyes and the sketch lines unpainted. Add a thin line of black between the wings using a liner brush for a clean line. But don't worry if your line is crooked; you can always touch it up with the wing colors after it dries.

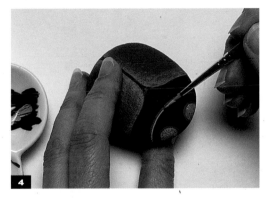

Step Four Using the round brush, add highlights around the eyes and between the body and the head. First paint a dark gray line (by mixing black and white); then add a thinner, lighter gray line over the edge. Mistakes are no problem—when dry, simply paint over the unwanted portions with black and try again.

Step Five Paint the pupils with sap green, and use phthalo blue for the irises. Dot in white highlights with the tip of the round or liner brush. Paint one large highlight and a smaller one just below it for realistic-looking eyes.

Step Six Sketch the spots (or the beetle's stripes) with a colored pencil. Use a circle template if you aren't happy with your hand-drawn circles. Ladybug spots are usually symmetrical, but they certainly don't have to be. Be creative and try something different, like heart-shaped spots! First line the outer edges of the spots with black, and then fill in the centers.

Step Seven Sketch the symmetrical ladybug body markings with a white colored pencil, and then use white paint to fill them in. Some beetles are vividly marked, so you can get really inventive with markings and colors and still create authentic-looking insects. To get even more ideas for your beetles, look for examples in an encyclopedia or on the Internet.

Step Eight Glue a small, extra-strong magnet onto the underside of the ladybug. When the magnet is set, glue on the antennae by placing a small drop of glue on the underside near the eyes and setting the wires into the glue. (I like black 24-gauge craft wire.) To form different shapes, twist the wire around a brush stem or other round object. Prop up the rock with folded paper so the ends of the antennae rest on the table while they dry.

Step Nine When the paint is dry, your ladybug will make an attractive refrigerator magnet—to keep on display or to give away! Though these painted rocks need to remain small so that the magnets can hold their weight, it doesn't mean that your options are limited. Small buds and bugs offer you limitless possibilities for exploring color and design. Take a hike for inspiration; you'll be in the perfect place for observing nature—and gathering supplies.

PAINTING FLOWERS

Before painting these flowers, make sure you are familiar with the painting techniques demonstrated on page 7.

Rose Cover the rock with a dark base, such as black or burnt umber. Transfer the design (below) with a white pencil. Using the round brush, paint the petals with a medium color, leaving some background showing between the petals. Add highlights and shadowed edges to the petals with wet layering.

Daisy Sketch the center and some radiating lines. Use the round brush for the petals—press down first; then quickly lift the brush to taper off the stroke toward the center. Paint the center with a medium color, and then shade the bottom edge.

Forget-Me-Not Sketch the center and five short radiating lines. Load the flat brush with white and purple (mix blue and red), and make blended C strokes around the center. To finish, stipple yellow dots in the center.

Lily Double-load the round brush with white and yellow. Make one stroke, touching lightly, then lift up gently as you move along the line of

the petal. Turn the brush over and repeat, butting yellow against the yellow of the first stroke and starting and finishing at the end points. Stipple the petals with orange, and add green stamen lines with yellow pollen sacs at their tips.

Sunflower Sketch a large center with small triangular petals around it. Use the round brush to paint each petal yellow. Add orange with small, feathered strokes—starting from the center to halfway up the petal. Repeat with red, painting only one third of the way up the petal. Paint the center black or burnt umber. Stipple orange into a ring inside the center; then finish by stippling yellow over that.

SUMMER LANDSCAPE ON STONE: EASY LANDSCAPE TECHNIQUES

Outdoor scenes are common painting subjects, but a landscape on rock is entirely unique. Rock and stone are the perfect canvases, since they are a natural part of almost any landscape. And the infinite variety of shapes and textures adds further interest to any painting. I'll show you the simple techniques for capturing the elements in this country summer landscape, but don't limit yourself—explore all the possibilities. Whether a wild animal portrait or a vignette of flowers, whatever you like to paint would be equally lovely on a rock.

Summer Scenery This project uses the same painting techniques as any other rock or canvas painting, but it takes advantage of the rock's surface texture to add visual interest. You can see how the naturally rugged edges of the flagstone complement the beauty of this pastoral scene.

Step One Any of these rocks would make a good landscape painting, but I chose thin flagstone so that I could display it on an easel. Shown in the background are two natural field rocks that are equally suited for landscape painting; each has a flat side for standing the rock upright. You may also purchase thicker flagstone with layered edges that can be left unpainted for added effect. Wash the flagstone well to remove any loose layers that could easily chip off during painting.

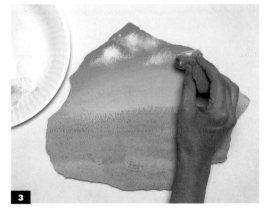

Step Two Begin by painting the sky with the flat brush, starting with light blue (mix white and phthalo blue) at the top and making wide, sweeping strokes. If your brush skips, wet it with a little water, but not so much that you can't achieve good coverage. While the paint is still wet, double-load the brush, dipping it first in blue and then in white. Then hold the brush with the blue at the top and stroke back and forth until the colors begin to blend well. Keep moving down, adding more white to the brush, until you reach about halfway down the rock.

Step Three While the sky is still wet, sponge on clouds. To do this, squeeze the sponge between your fingers to pull back the angled edges. Dip the sponge in white, and then dab it on paper until the paint is worked into the sponge and the excess is removed. Gently sponge on the clouds, beginning with the larger clouds at the top and working down to the smaller, thinner ones at the horizon. Remember to make the clouds denser in the middle and thinner at the edges.

Step Four To paint the distant hills over the bottom portion of the sky, double-load your clean flat brush with purple (red mixed with blue) and white. With the purple at the top, make a long, curving stroke, going back over it until it is softly blended. Then paint the next nearest hill just below it the same way. You may paint multiple, overlapping hills if you want, but remember to leave the bottom half of the rock for the foreground.

Step Five Paint the distant slope of grass overlapping the nearest hill. Double-load the flat brush with light green (sap green and white) at the bottom and yellow mixed with white at the top. Using the same long strokes, add more light green as you paint farther down. Double-load the brush again with light green at the bottom and yellow mixed with white at the top. Paint the top of the foreground slope, overlapping the distant slope until blended. Then dip the brush in light green, and continue painting toward the bottom of the rock. Double-load the brush once more, this time with light green at the top and darker green at the bottom. Blend in the foreground at the bottom of the rock.

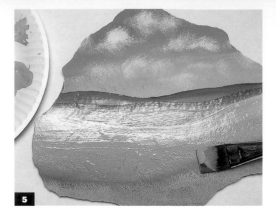

Step Six After the paint is dry, paint the barn with the flat brush. Place the barn just behind the foreground, partially hidden from view. Block in a gray roof, red front, and darker red side. Don't worry if you cut a bit into your foreground grass—you can touch it up later with white and yellow. Now, switching to the round brush and using a lighter gray, apply light, feathered strokes parallel to the roof slope to highlight the bottom half of the roof. Highlight the left side of the barn front with thin, vertical strokes of orange mixed with white. Continue across the front with a few more random vertical strokes to simulate the look of boards.

Step Seven Next paint approximately four black horizontal lines on the roof with the edge of the flat brush. Switch to a liner brush and paint a black line under the roof edge along the side and under the front peak. Feather in some light, vertical black lines on the barn side. Paint the front window black. Add white highlight lines just above the black lines at the roof edge along the sides and the peak. Then add thin white lines for the trim around the window and the barn door detail.

Step Eight Paint the tree trunks and branches with burnt umber or dark gray and the round brush. Stroke from the base upward, tapering off at the top and the ends of the branches. Use black to shade one side of each trunk and the underside of each branch. Make the foreground tree appear closer by placing it lower than the other trees and making it taller.

Step Nine Using the round brush, paint the tree and foliage with dark green (green mixed with touches of burnt umber and phthalo blue). Holding the brush vertically, lightly and repeatedly dab the bristles on the rock. (I use old brushes, since this can damage the bristles.) Move around the branches randomly, leaving some areas open and tapering off toward the edges. Paint the bushes the same way, making them denser at the bottom. (The distant bushes may require a smaller round brush.) Use light green to randomly paint highlights on the trees and bushes, letting the darker green show through. Then add white and a few more highlights in selected areas. If you cover too much of your foliage with highlights, you can always add more of the dark green later.

Step Ten Using a liner brush and thinned black, paint the thicker vertical fence posts; then connect the posts with thin lines. Taper off into the foreground tree and wherever the fence disappears—either behind the hill or barn. Highlight the tops and sides of the fence and posts with thinned white, staying consistent with the light source. Use dark green to drybrush tufts of grass into the foreground and around the bases of the foreground tree and bushes. Begin with the foreground and work up, so your brush is dryer as you apply the shorter distant tufts. Next paint the long grasses in the foreground by making quick, overlapping curved strokes—first with dark green, then with white mixed with yellow.

Step Eleven When you've completed this charming scene, you can display it in a small tabletop easel or hang it in a plate holder. If you decide to put your piece on view without a display, be sure to glue some felt to the bottom to prevent scratching your furniture.

MONOGRAM PAPERWEIGHTS: LETTERING TECHNIQUES

Rocks make superb paperweights, and a hand-painted, classic monogram design is a stylish addition to any desktop, whether it be at the office or in your own home. A rock paperweight that you have hand-lettered with your favorite inspirational saying makes a thoughtful gift or a useful affirmation for yourself. For this project, I will show you different ways to letter, from simple to ornate. Then you can experiment with different fonts and styles and choose the ones you like best.

Perfect Paperweights To master the lettering techniques in this project, you'll want to choose smooth, flat rocks with no pits or ridges. The three techniques are lettering on bare rock with a permanent marker, lettering on a painted rock with paint markers, and lettering a monogram with paints and brushes.

Marker Step One When lettering on bare rock, I recommend using an extra-fine permanent marker for better control. Before you start, make sure your marker has a good point and that the ink flows freely. First transfer your letters onto the bare rock using carbon paper, but keep the design nearby for reference. Use a light touch and keep the marker moving; the ink may bleed if you press in one place for too long.

Paint Marker Step One To letter on a painted rock with paint markers, first apply your base color with the flat brush. Permanent, fine-point paint markers (found in art, craft, and office supply stores) come in a variety of colors, including gold and silver metallics. If you're going to use a gold or light-colored paint marker, choose a dark background color, such as black, for contrast. You may want to work out your color schemes beforehand to make sure you are happy with them. You may also want to consider favorite colors, a family crest, or the color of your office décor when choosing your color palette.

Paint Marker Step Two Transfer your design with a white pencil. Then use a metallic paint marker to paint the center initial and the surrounding leaf sprays; keep the marker moving and use a light touch for best results. When the metallic color is dry, touch up any mistakes with your background color. Because the paint in the markers flows out thinly, I do not recommend trying fine details. To keep the paint from bleeding into crevices, never hold the pen in place while it's depressed, and use it only on smooth surfaces.

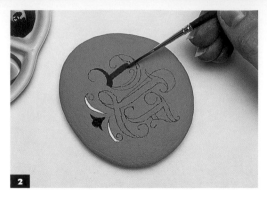

Paintbrush Step One For a monogram design with three initials, print out or photocopy the middle initial so it's larger than the other two. Draw guidelines on tracing paper and trace over your letters, adjusting the letters and flourishes so they fit together. If you don't have tracing paper, cut out your letters and sketch around them to work out your design.

Paintbrush Step Two Transfer your design onto the rock with colored pencil (it is least likely to smudge on the paint). If you decide to use carbon paper to transfer your design, be careful not to press too hard. When the transfer is finished, lift the carbon paper off the rock without allowing it to slide. Then use a liner brush to fill in the wide portions of the letters and the flourish with color.

Paintbrush Step Three Outline the design with black, keeping the brush tip tapered and clear of buildup. Create the swirls in parts, always pulling the brush toward you. I prefer to outline a curve from the inside while pivoting my hand. I also use a magnifying headset (found at art supply stores) for detail work like this.

Paintbrush Final Step Once you've finished working on these functional and attractive paperweights, be sure to seal them carefully before displaying them or giving them away. (See "Clear-Coating the Finished Piece" below.) You can also finish the backs with small self-adhesive felt pieces, available at art and craft supply stores.

CLEAR-COATING THE FINISHED PIECE

A glossy clear coat will enliven and enhance color enormously. Enrich and protect your rock creations at the same time with a permanent, waterproof, clear acrylic spray-finish. A light coating is all you need. For serious water- and weatherproofing, spray several light coats. (Consult the specific directions for the brand you choose.)

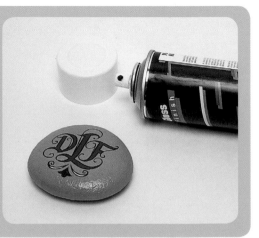

PAPERWEIGHT DESIGN TEMPLATES

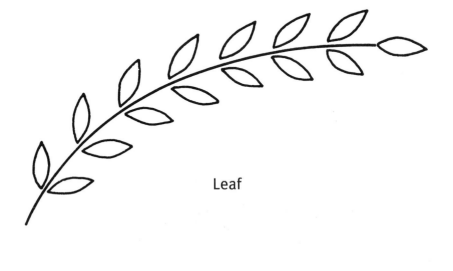

Leaf

Flourish

There are numerous fonts you can use for your monograms. For examples, try the lettering styles from a computer word processing program, or search the Internet for alternatives.

SWEET ILLUSIONS: USING 3-D FABRIC PAINT

Pick up a chocolate and marvel at it—but don't bite into it! Display these luscious-looking rock candies as a conversational "appetizer." The good news about these chocolates is how easy they are to create; almost any small rock will do. Just make sure you choose rocks that are relatively equal in size. The fun part of this project is creating the delectable candy decorations. But don't worry about being too decadent—chocolate has never had fewer calories!

Rock Candy These chocolates are decorated with 3-D fabric paint, which can be purchased in art and craft supply stores. Squeezing the paint out of a bottle is very much like decorating a cake with icing, and it looks remarkably the same.

Step One Paint the chocolate base colors on your selected candy-shaped rocks. (Rough-textured rocks are fine, but any large pits should be smoothed with wood filler.) Several coats of paint (at least two for dark chocolate, and three or more for milk and white) will be required to obtain the distinct chocolate look. Place a piece of paper under the rock to make it easier to turn, and use a toothpick to steady the rock while you're painting. If you want to paint the bottoms, wait until one side is thoroughly dry before turning the rock over. You can also use a hair dryer to speed up the drying time.

Step Two Practice using the 3-D paint squeeze bottles on paper before you begin decorating. Hold the bottle upside down, and gently shake it to get the paint to flow to the tip. Then squeeze carefully until the paint comes out. Maintain even pressure on the bottle as you work, and keep a towel handy to wipe off any paint that builds up on the tip. For a red rose, start in the middle of the spiral. Hold the bottle upright and move outward without overlapping the lines. Paint the pink flower in strokes, one petal at a time. Paint toward the stem and lift off at the end as you release the pressure on the bottle.

Step Three Paint the rose leaves using two side-by-side strokes, painting toward the rose and lifting off at the end as you release pressure on the bottle. For the pink flower, use the same one-stroke method to paint the two small leaves at its base. To keep the paint flowing smoothly, remember to occasionally shake the paint down to the tip of the bottle. Then paint the stem, moving your whole hand steadily as you draw the line down to the leaves. Paint the stem leaves last, also with one stroke each. To minimize the risk of smearing the paint, let the paint dry between painting the flower, the stem, and the leaves.

Step Four For the milk chocolate decorations, swirl on a plain brown 3-D color. I also found a slightly darker "hot chocolate" color that I used on the white chocolate candy. You may want to experiment with different browns to discover what looks best. The decoration designs shown here are typical of chocolate candies; you can also let the natural rock shape suggest a design. Visit a chocolatier website or store for additional references.

Step Five To match your chocolate base color with a 3-D color, paint over the 3-D paint with your base color. (Black 3-D paint may work as well.) For the square milk chocolate candy, paint the bottom half with the dark chocolate color to simulate a half-dipped candy. Then paint the decoration with a brown 3-D paint. When this is dry, use a liner brush to paint over the 3-D paint with the dark chocolate color.

6

7

Step Six This white chocolate design is done with cream 3-D paint (off-white and cream colors are best for the look of white chocolate). Draw parallel lines across the candy, each with a dip in the middle. Work quickly so the paint lines stay wet and pliable. Then run a toothpick down the middle, pulling the paint down. This technique works best when done on a flat, smooth surface.

Step Seven To create the appearance of a sprinkling of ground nuts, dot the rocks with various-sized spots of cream 3-D paint (or any off-white color). When this dries, paint the nuts with an orange and brown mixture to simulate the nut skins. Paint the skins on only some of the nuts, and vary the coverage randomly from just one side to the entire top. This will mimic the way real nut pieces look.

8

Step Eight Now that you have a variety of sweet designs, arrange a balanced group that shows off your assortment of decorations. If you really want to fool your family or friends, try displaying your faux candy creations in a candy dish or in candy papers (as shown on page 24).

27

HIDDEN-MESSAGE ANGELS: DRYBRUSHING TECHNIQUES

Angels are a popular artistic theme, and a hidden message painted on the underside of the rock makes this painted angel an enchanting personalized gift. Choose a rock large enough to hold a detailed portrait yet light enough to pick up and turn over easily. The rock must also be large enough to write your hidden message, which could be an inspirational saying or a favorite prayer. You can transfer calligraphic letters, or use your own handwriting to convey a personal touch.

Angelic Messages For this project, I used a drybrush technique to render the soft textures of hair and feathers.

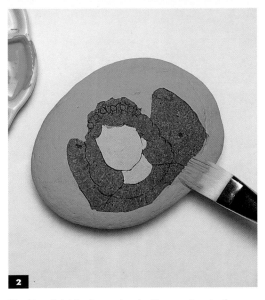

Step One Carefully transfer your choice of angel design (see page 33) onto a bare rock using carbon paper. Center the design on the rock, leaving room for the border at the bottom. Transfer just the outlines of the design; not the face or wing details. You can indicate where the roses in the hair will be by drawing circles.

Step Two Paint the face and neck with several coats of a flesh color (orange mixed with white), but leave the chin line unpainted. Mix a sky blue color (phthalo blue and white), and paint the background with a flat brush. Imagine where the row of roses will come across the bottom, and paint the blue up to that line. After the paint is dry, turn the rock over and paint the back with the same blue mixture.

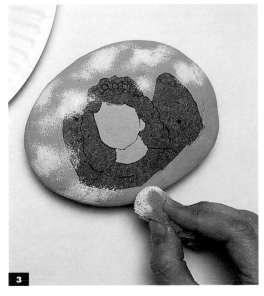

Step Three Grip a sponge so that the end is small and rounded and the edges are pulled back out of the way. Dip the sponge in white paint, and dab it on paper until the excess paint is removed. Then gently dab the sponge onto the blue sky to create the small cottonlike clouds around the angel's head. For added softness, let the sponged clouds bleed into the angel design where they overlap. When the paint is dry, turn the rock over, and continue sponging clouds all over the back of the rock.

Step Four Sketch or transfer the face onto the painted rock using a black pencil. Paint the whites and the irises of the eyes, and apply the lip color with red lightened with a touch of white. Use the wet layering technique to add a light blush of cheek color (flesh with a touch of red), and then drybrush a slightly darker blush over the top and in the middle. Use light, feathered strokes, and slowly build up the color. Don't worry if you paint outside of the face edge; the hair will cover this up.

Step Five Drybrush the contours of the face and neck with burnt umber, using light, feathered strokes to build up the color. Try "scrubbing" the brush tips very gently to produce an even texture; make sure the brush is fairly dry, as wet paint will produce a solid coverage. Lightly drybrush around the edge of the face and neck, and add a thin shadow just above the gown. Switch to a liner brush loaded with burnt umber darkened with black. With light strokes, detail the eyes, the eyebrows, the nostrils, the division between the lips, and the chin line. In each eye, paint a black pupil with a white highlight next to it. Then highlight the nose line, upper lip, and chin with white.

Step Six Paint the wings with beige (white mixed with a touch of burnt umber). When the wings are dry, lightly sketch or transfer the feather details. Drybrush the feather details and the outside wing edges with medium burnt umber. Then drybrush highlights on the wing feathers and across the apex of each wing with white. Use light strokes, building up the color until you achieve the desired highlights. Then drybrush pink shadows into the inner areas of the wings (next to the hair) using a soft scrubbing motion.

Step Seven Next paint the medium base color of the hair. When it's dry, drybrush the hair shadows with burnt umber mixed with a touch of black, paying close attention to the area around the face and beside the neck. The brush can be wetter for these strokes, but make sure that the bristles are splayed to give the appearance of individual hairs. Mix the highlight color by adding white and yellow to your base hair color, and then drybrush the hair highlights the same way you did the hair shadows. Remember that you want to paint multiple lines rather than texture, which is done with a drier brush. Work the highlights into the areas above and below the roses to create a contrasting background.

Step Eight Use several coats of cream (white and a touch of yellow) to paint the gown. When it's dry, drybrush pink along the neckline, across the area where the bottom row of pearls will be, and across the shoulders. Be sure to gradually lighten the color toward the cream center. Add touches of burnt umber to the pink to create a dark mauve, and use it to drybrush along the edges of the shoulders.

Step Nine Using the tip of a liner brush, dot on the pearls with white. Take your time, and reload the brush often—but not too generously or the heavy paint will produce a blob instead of a dot. Try to make the dots as consistent in size as possible. Next paint the two button shadows with dark mauve, and then dot on the buttons over the shadows with pink.

Step Ten Sketch the roses at the top and along the bottom of the rock by drawing simple circles. Draw three at the top, with a slightly larger one in the center. Vary the sizes, and place some roses higher than others along the bottom. Keep in mind that you will eventually cover up the transition between the dress and the sky, but don't worry about this now; if needed, you can apply color later to complete this effect.

Step Eleven Paint the leaves and the areas between the roses with dark green (green mixed with touches of burnt umber and phthalo blue). Don't worry about painting the roses at this time; this will be done later. Try to vary the sizes and directions of the leaves, and keep some areas open to create more interest and movement. Then paint all the rose circles with dark red (red mixed with burnt umber). Don't forget to paint the leaves for the spray of roses in the angel's hair!

12

13

Step Twelve Define the leaves by lightly painting highlights with light green (green mixed with white). Just a few light strokes with the round or liner brush in the middle of a leaf is enough. Do not highlight between the roses—a dark background is best for contrast with the highlighted edges of the petals. There's no need to highlight any leaves that recede in the design or are very small.

Step Thirteen Use a liner brush to paint the rose petals with dark pink. Leave the dark red background showing between the petals, and don't worry if the petals merge occasionally. Then highlight the outer edges of the petals with light pink. Use a slightly wavy line to mimic real petal edges. Keep the brush tip clear of buildup and lightly loaded with paint to produce a clear highlight line.

14

15

Step Fourteen When the portrait is thoroughly dry, turn the rock over and transfer your message (or lightly sketch it with a pencil in your own handwriting). Paint the message with a liner brush, referring to the original type for details. Touch up any mistakes with the original sky color and white.

Step Fifteen When the lettering is dry, add any finishing touches to the portrait you feel are necessary. To enhance the bright colors of your angelic creation, you can brush on a glossy acrylic sealer for a high sheen, or spray them with acrylic sealant. (See page 22.)

PRESERVING MIXED COLORS

I often need to preserve my mixed colors for later use while waiting for a painting to dry. Because acrylic paint darkens when it dries, it's difficult to match a previously mixed color. The solution is to preserve the mixed colors with plastic wrap. Simply wrap it over your palette and uncover it when you are ready to paint again.

ANGEL TEMPLATES

Angels

Roses

BOOKENDS WRITTEN IN STONE: WORKING WITH NATURAL SHAPES

Lend charm and interest to your bookcase with a set of stone bookends. Large rocks are best for this project because they're heavy enough to remain anchored. Look for rocks that are close to square in shape, but remember that they don't have to be flawless. Their bumps and imperfections will work with and enhance the design. Look for spine decoration ideas on your own bookshelves; vintage books are also a wonderful source of inspiration.

Rock Solid Bookends One bookend is painted on a square piece of flagstone purchased from a rock supplier; the other is natural rock from a desert wash. The tilted angles and imperfect contours of the natural rock just add to the charm of this project.

Step One When you're rock hunting for this project, consider that the book-end must stand up, so it needs a fairly flat bottom (although you can make some adjustments with wood filler) and a vaguely square side for the spines. Begin by sketching the design with a colored pencil, using any obvious ridge or crevice on the spine side or along the top as a division between the books. A bump or ridge on the cover flap side can be used to place a bookmark tassel. Sketch your design all the way around the five sides of the bookend "cube," leaving only the bottom bare.

Step Two Paint black outlines for the general design to indicate the divisions between the books and the division between the covers and the pages. Don't worry if your lines aren't perfectly straight. Paint the outlines up to the bookmark tassel and into it a bit, but don't outline the bookmark.

Step Three On the five sides to be painted, block in the base colors for the covers and pages, leaving a thin portion of the black outline showing. When this is dry, turn the rock over and continue the colors around the bottom edges. Use the round or liner brush when painting next to the outline, and hold it upright when negotiating over bumps and pits to keep your edges relatively straight. (Don't worry if you cover part of the black outline; you can repaint it later.) Use the flat brush to cover the large areas. I used a cream color (white with a touch of yellow) for the "pages," but remember that the pages and any light "cover" colors will require more than one coat.

Step Four Next mix a darker version of your cover colors to paint thin shadows between the book covers, butting the shadows up against the black outline. Mix a little black and burnt umber into the cream, and add a shadow line to the page edges. When painting on a raised surface, it's a good idea to prop your painting hand on your free hand, rather than on an unsteady rock surface.

Step Five Using the cream shadow color, paint the marquise-shaped gap between the pages where the tassel emerges. Then shade the inside of the gap with black. Using black, block in a shadow along one side and underneath the tassel (but not the string portion that connects the ball to the page split). Using light strokes, feather the edge of the shadow to soften it.

Step Six Block in the base color of the bookmark tassel. Then paint two strings emerging from the pages and connecting to the tassel ball. For interest, don't make the strings too uniform. Then mix a darker color, and outline each string with a liner brush, making the shadow side thicker. Detail the tassel with lines to indicate the separations of the strings. Further enhance the realism by adding spots of black where the strings overlap and at the bottom of the tassel ball.

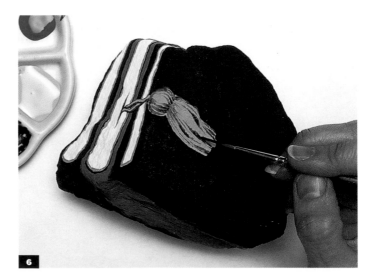

Step Seven Next highlight the tassel with white lines to add dimension, but don't cover the green base color completely. Then paint a thin highlight line around the cover edge of each "book" where it surrounds the pages. Use a lighter version of the book cover base instead of white for this subtle highlight. For example, try painting a red highlight on a maroon book or a lavender highlight on a purple one.

Step Eight Pencil in the spine decorations, and then paint them carefully with a liner brush. Take your time and go slowly, paying close attention to dips and pits and in the rock and keeping the brush upright. Where the spine decoration falls in the shaded area between the books, shade the decoration as well, matching it to the cover shadow.

Step Nine When you're finished, set the rock on its unpainted base, and let it dry thoroughly overnight. Paint the other bookend the same way, changing the colors and decorations if you like. Try painting the spines with different lettering styles to capture the look of a particular period. Or you might even want to letter your books with your own clever titles!

MAINTAINING A REFERENCE LIBRARY

References are indispensable to an artist. I have accumulated a large source library over the years, including extensive wildlife references. Even if you want to paint imaginative, stylized subjects, looking at examples still helps spark inspiration. Books are not the only source for ideas; you can also search the Internet for many useful references.

PICTURESQUE CACTUS GARDEN: CREATING DIMENSION

This colorful lizard looks so real, you almost expect it to jump off the rock and scurry into the bushes! This type of realistic dimension is easy to replicate with proper highlights and shadows, which you'll learn to create in this project. I'll also show you how to paint these charming little pueblo dwellings; the adobe look makes them a natural addition to a cactus garden. If you don't grow cacti, little cottages would be equally delightful among your houseplants.

Cactus Garden Complements This project uses a combination of wet layering and drybrushing techniques to add dimension. If you prefer, you can try painting a snake instead of a lizard using the same techniques.

Step One Choose a smooth rock for the lizard, and transfer the pattern from page 43 using carbon paper. You may need to adjust the tail position to fit your rock. After you determine where your light source is, paint a solid black shadow underneath the lizard directly opposite the light source. Also consider which body parts are closer to the rock and which parts are lifted, such as the tail end and the head; the body parts closer to the rock will have thinner, closer cast shadows. Since the tail end is meant to look as though it is raised, its shadow will be some distance away rather than touching the tail. The shadow for the head will sit away from the head in the same way. Once the shadows are painted, drybrush them to feather the edges.

Step Two Block in the base lizard color, leaving the guidelines at the tops of the legs, the back edge, the eye, and the ear uncovered. (Leave the eye unpainted for now.) Choose a color that contrasts with your rock, such as the green I've used here. Use a liner brush for the outline, the feet, and the tail, and then fill in these areas with the round brush.

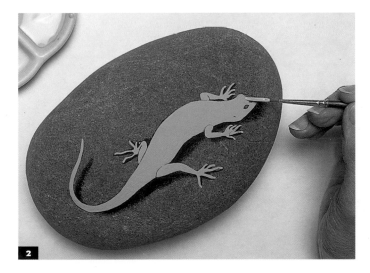

Step Three Wet layer the shadow along the sides of the body with the round brush and dark green (green mixed with touches of burnt umber and phthalo blue). Leave a line of the lighter green showing at the bottom shadowed side. Shade the top of the head and the bottom of the cheek with light, feathered strokes. Using a liner brush, paint shadows on the legs, the toes, and along the tail. With a darker green, drybrush the shaded ridge above the eye. Dot in the ear and deepen the shaded areas along the top, the tail, and in front of the bottom back leg with the darker green.

Step Four Using the round brush, drybrush white highlights with light, feathered strokes, building up the highlights gradually as you go. Highlight along the lizard's body, on the thick part of the tail, and above the ridge of the eye. Then switch to a liner brush and continue highlighting the smaller areas: the end of the tail, the bottom "cheek," the tops of the legs, and the feet just above the toes. Next paint a thin, white highlight above and below the eye and another highlight above the ear.

Step Five Paint the eye black and add a red highlight in the middle with a liner brush. Now take a moment to look over your lizard. This is the time to enhance the shadows and highlights or straighten up an outline before the final pattern is painted. Remember that a highlight will be more intense in the center and fade toward the edge. You may also want to accentuate the highlights at the elbows and knees, along the center of the body, or on the lifted portion of the tail. Paint subtle highlights and build the color gradually.

Step Six Paint the black pattern using a series of rough spots of varying sizes, making them heavily concentrated at the head, largest along the body, and tapered to small stripelike spots along the tail. Fade out the pattern toward the bottom of the body, and add some small spots to the tops of the legs. There are countless ways to paint reptile skin; consult an encyclopedia or the Internet for more color and pattern ideas.

Step Seven For the adobe dwellings, choose roughly square or rectangular rocks. Many rocks (such as the ones shown here) have square chunks cut out of them, which works perfectly for the pueblo look. Mix a base adobe color with beige (white mixed with a touch of burnt umber), orange, and dabs of red and white. Use the flat brush to cover the rock generously, filling any crevices. You don't have to paint the bottom, but be sure to paint down around the bottom edges.

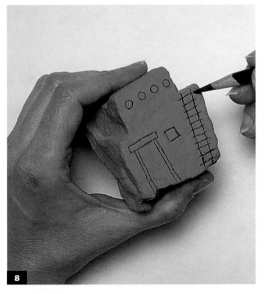

Step Eight When the base coat is thoroughly dry, sketch the pueblo design with a black colored pencil. Include elements such as a pole-topped door, small square windows, a line of protruding roof poles, pots leaning against the sides, and the distinctive pole ladders that lead to the roof. You certainly don't have to copy the design exactly as shown here; feel free to be creative and come up with your own unique designs.

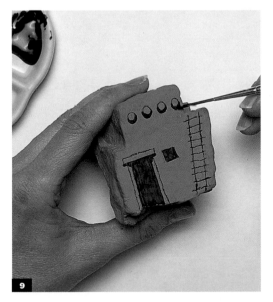

Step Nine Using a liner brush, paint the door and the pole shadow above it, the window next to the door, and the shadows underneath the roof poles. You don't need to drybrush any of the shadows; just color them with wet paint. Leave enough space between elements—such as between the door and the window—so that you have room to paint the frames.

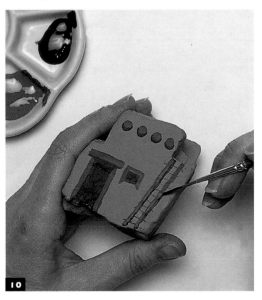

Step Ten Paint the roof poles, the sides and top of the window frame (which is actually a recessed square hole), and the sides of the door frame (also a recess). Use a color dark enough to contrast with the base color, yet light enough to contrast with the black shadows. Then paint the side poles of the ladder, shading them on one side with a line of black.

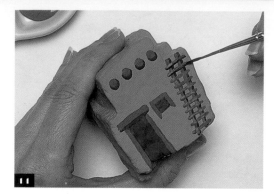

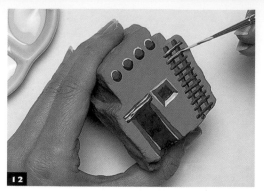

Step Eleven When the side poles of the ladder are dry, paint the rungs using the same color. Keep in mind that the rungs extend slightly past the side poles. Paint shadows along the undersides of the rungs with black. Then check the shadow at the top of the door, underneath the pole; make sure it angles down over the door as shown in the example. Before moving on to the highlights, step back and assess the shadows, making any necessary adjustments.

Step Twelve For the highlights, use a beige light enough to contrast with the base adobe color. Add thin highlights on each roof pole, the tops of the ladder rungs, the inside bottom of the door frame, and the pole over the door. Paint the bottom of the window, and add a thin highlight over the top. Then use white to accentuate the highlights in a few places, such as the outside edge of the bottom of the window frame and the pole over the door.

Step Thirteen For the final steps, paint the details on the side of the dwelling, such as additional windows and the adobe pot I've shown in my example. (See "Adobe Pot" below.) Try painting several of the adobe dwellings using rocks of varying sizes and shapes. Add various details to the front and sides, such as a thorny cactus or old water barrel. Then arrange your own southwestern scene with your lizard rock and adobe dwellings!

ADOBE POT

To paint an adobe pot, first block in a light beige base color, leaving the opening un-painted. Then drybrush a highlight in the center of the pot with white. Use black to paint the opening of the pot and the shadow around it. For the shadow, use light, feath-ered strokes that are thicker at the bottom and taper off toward the top. When this is dry, sketch the pot design, referring to the patterns on page 43. If your pot is too small for fine detail, just add a stripe or two. Then outline the pot design with black and accent it with red.

SOUTHWESTERN TEMPLATES

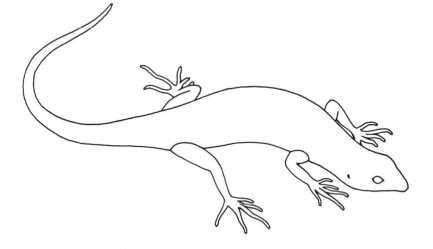

Lizard

Adobe Pots

BIRD BATH:
PAINTING BIRDS AND FISH

Brilliantly colored birds and fish are beautiful to look at and fun to paint. Fish can be adapted to almost any rock, but it's exciting when you discover perfect fish shapes. The best bird-shaped rocks are round at the head and thinner toward the tail feathers, although simple oval rocks can work as well. When you see how fun and easy these adorable animals are to create, you'll want to make a whole school of fish and an entire flock of birds!

Fanciful Fish Feather and fin detailing, brilliant colors, and the right rocks bring this bird bath to life. You'll also need to find a suitable container to house your fish, such as this natural-looking stone bowl.

Step One The rock shown here is an excellent shape for a sparrow: The back curves slightly, the head is round, and the belly protrudes. Using the flat brush, cover the rock with a beige base coat. When it's dry, lightly draw the sparrow with a colored pencil (or transfer the pattern on page 47). The length of the wings and tail feathers will depend on the shape of your rock, but always keep the eyes and beak fairly close to the top of the head. Using a liner brush and black paint, outline the entire design. (For the bluebird, use blues instead of browns and exclude the orange patches, orange crest, and white-tipped feathers.)

Step Two Fill in the eye with black. Then use a liner brush loaded with burnt umber to paint a thin shadow at the sparrow's neck with thin, short strokes. Add a fine line inside the upper and lower outlines of the beak. Cover the crest of the head with a bright orange (red mixed with yellow), starting at the middle of the beak and tapering down between the top of the wings. Add a triangular orange patch that extends from each wing into the upper chest. Use white to cover the rest of the chest and head with thin, short strokes, but leave enough space between the strokes for the beige to show through.

Step Three Add a touch of black to burnt umber to create a darker brown, and use this color to paint feathered strokes into the orange crest, concentrating more at the beak and at the tops of the sparrow's wings. Add a dark burnt umber strip from the beak to the eye, and then taper it just past the eye as it extends toward the back of the head. Add some soft, downy feathers at the tops of the wings with dark burnt umber, and add outlines inside the black throughout the wing feathers.

Step Four Add white to burnt umber and highlight the bottom edge of the upper beak, the middles of each claw, and the tops of the wings. Use the same color to paint the nostrils and thin diagonal lines on the side of each feather. Paint a fine white outline around each eye, and highlight each eye with two dots of white: one large and one small. Paint solid white tips on the top two rows of wing feathers, and add a few strokes of orange on the tops of the wings.

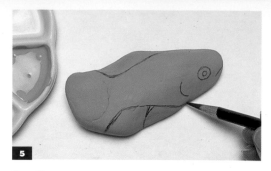

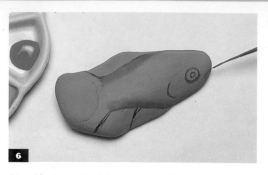

Step Five For the fish, first cover the rock with a base coat. (I used medium green.) Let it dry completely, and then sketch the design on your chosen rock with a colored pencil. Use the natural contours of the rock as a guide for your design, and refer to an encyclopedia or the Internet for types of fish to copy.

Step Six Double-load the flat brush with medium green and blue-green. Paint a shadow along the top and bottom of the body, flipping the brush so that blue-green is always on the outside. Switch to a liner brush and paint blue-green lines at the gill, the mouth, and around the eye; paint a thicker shadow line under the eye.

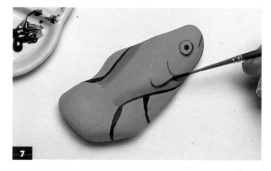

Step Seven Paint black outlines around the fins, and define the top and bottom of the body. Paint black spaces between the fins where they separate. Paint the eyeball black, and define the shadow underneath the eye with a thin black line inside the blue-green. Lightly pencil in the shape of the side fin, and then drybrush a dark shadow underneath it with black.

Step Eight I used red to paint the body markings, which is somewhat translucent, so I loaded the brush generously for solid coverage. Using long, tapered strokes that move toward the body, paint red lines on all the fins. Make sure to leave enough room between these strokes for another set of lines. (Refer to the template on page 47 to see how the lines meet from either side.)

Step Nine With a mix of yellow and white, paint the second set of fin lines between the first red set. Then paint the side fin lines, tapering them toward the gill. Paint around the eye with the yellow-white, and add a white highlight on the side of the pupil.

Step Ten If the fish rocks will be in water, spray them first with several coats of clear acrylic sealer. (It's also a good idea to seal the bird rocks if they will be displayed outdoors.) Then you can place the fish in a shallow pond or find a special outdoor perch for your new feathered friends!

SPARROW AND FISH TEMPLATES

Side

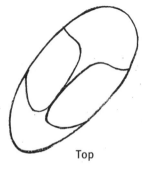
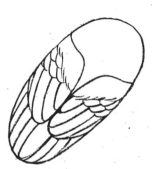

Top

Bird

Top

Side

Side

Side

Fish

NOAH'S ARK: PAINTING SMALL

Tiny animals capture the heart in a big way. To create a cohesive look for Noah and his animals, try to choose very smooth rocks of the same relative size. The key to painting small areas and fine details is to use a light touch with the brush and to simplify the techniques. For this project, I painted five miniature creatures, but you can try others as well—after all, the ark supposedly housed them all!

Menagerie at Sea You'll need small liner brushes to create these lifelike little creatures, but the techniques aren't new. Just follow the steps to create your own menagerie!

Step One Moving clockwise from the top left, you can see the rocks I chose for the bear, hippopotamus, tiger, pig, and elephant. If a rock is unstable, use wood filler first to create a flat base. To begin, paint the base colors on each rock. For the elephant, hippopotamus, and pig, choose a medium color that can be shaded with a darker tone and highlighted with a lighter one. Paint the bear black. For the tiger, use a yellow-orange beige. Lay each rock on a piece of paper for easy turning and moving, and use a toothpick to steady the rock while painting. With the tip of a liner brush and a light touch, paint the black outline designs of all of the animals but the bear. (See the animal templates on page 53.) Fill in the shadowed areas, such as underneath the elephant and between the tiger's front legs and under its front paws, but don't fill in the tiger's eyes.

Step Two Mix a dark gray (black with a bit of white) and paint shadows on the elephant, defining its contours, wrinkling the ears, and rounding the underbelly, legs, and head. Add horizontal wrinkles to the trunk. Mix a light gray (add more white to black) and use it to add highlights (including the tail). Paint the tusks white, and add a tiny white dot in each eye. Keep your strokes especially light when painting the highlights. Try to use just the tip of the brush, and make sure to keep the paint fresh and the brush free of buildup.

3

4

Step Three Using short, small strokes, paint the white fur on the tiger around the eyes, the muzzle, the sides of the head, the chest, the insides of the front legs, the toes, and the perimeter of the haunches. Add white fur to the insides of the ears and the end of the tail. Be careful not to touch the wet paint as you turn the rock to paint the other side. If you want, use a hair dryer to speed up the drying time.

Step Four Paint the light pink nose in the shape of a fat letter T, leaving some black around it. Mix an orange-brown that's darker than the base, and paint tiny hairs over the base color. Then shade the neck below the jaw. Using black, paint the body stripes and markings. Follow the typical tiger pattern shown, using short strokes. Finish by adding a black dot to each eye just below the upper lid.

Step Five I chose a brownish-gray for the hippo to differentiate it from the elephant, but the painting technique is the same: Start with dark gray shadows, rounding the body, head, legs, and skin folds. Darken the insides of the ears, and add highlights with a light gray. Here I created a soft look by painting lines instead of a solid block. Next add a tiny white dot in each eye, spiked whiskers on the muzzle, tiny spiked hairs on the ears, and spiked fur on the end of the tail.

5

Step Six As you did for the hippo and the elephant, paint the pig's shadows first, mixing a reddish brown in the same tone as the pinkish base. Add spots to the body for interest, and paint them with lines rather than as solid blocks. Mix a lighter shade of the pinkish base for highlights. Carefully stipple in a highlight above each nostril, and highlight the head and body with short, light strokes to represent hairs. Switch to white and add a tiny dot to each eye, a few hairs at the top of the head, and a few hairs at the end of the tail.

6

Step Seven Using burnt umber mixed with a touch of white, build up the contours of the bear with short strokes. Always stroke in the direction the fur would normally grow. Leave black areas between the body parts, such as the muzzle, eyes, ears, head, and legs. When the paint is dry, either carefully remove the white pencil lines with a kneaded eraser or paint over them with black.

Step Eight Now paint the eyes and nose black. Build up the body fur with more short strokes of cream (white with a touch of yellow) or burnt umber mixed with more white. Don't use too much highlighting on the chest and belly; these areas are naturally in shadow. Build up the highlight at the end of the muzzle, leaving a vertical black line beneath the nose and another horizontal black line for the lips. Add a tiny white dot to each eye and to the nose.

Step Nine The rock shown here has a good ark shape, with a flat bottom for a base. It's a good idea to work out your ark design on paper before sketching it on the rock. Use the shape of the rock as a guide while you're designing, and make sure you include both a house and a barn portion. You may also want to add more animals peeking out from the barn and add trees and flowers for interest.

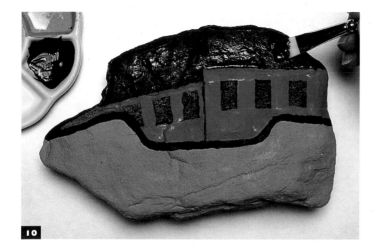

Step Ten Block in the base colors, leaving some space between colors where a guideline is needed. (I chose beige for the ark's base color, dark brownish-red for the roof, and a dark green for the buildings.) If you are painting both sides, continue the colors around to the back of the rock, but leave the windows unpainted. If you are painting only one side, be sure you paint far enough around the rock so that it can be viewed from the top or the side.

Step Eleven Outline the ark features and the lines above and below the trim with black. Fill in the windows and any areas inside the ark with black. Paint horizontal lines for the boards with dark brown (burnt umber with a touch of black); then alternate vertical lines for the boards' ends. Don't forget to add a few knotholes! Using long, tapering lines, apply burnt umber with a touch of white to shade the boards on both ends, and add a shadow line under the trim. Use green with a bit of black to shade under the roofs and above the trim; then define the house boards and barn. Paint a black checkerboard on the roofs, following the shapes of the rock and the roof.

Step Twelve Drybrush some cream highlights on the centers of the wooden boards on the body of the ark, following the same horizontal direction. Use red to highlight the trim, and define each of the roof tiles on three sides, tapering toward the tile tops. Highlight the house and the boards of the barn with light green (green mixed with white) lines. Then paint the trim on the windows white, but leave some black showing around the edges. Use soft touches of white to enhance some of the existing highlights, such as at the bottom of the roof line, at the edge of the house, and on spots on the trim.

Step Thirteen After you complete the ark and its furry inhabitants, set up an arrangement that shows them to their best advantage. You can prop up the ark and nestle the animals around it, or create clay bases to make the animals stand upright. You can even let them lie flat and observe them from a bird's-eye view as shown here—the choice is yours!

ANIMAL TEMPLATES

Here are basic designs for five different animals. Depending on the shapes of the rocks you find, adjust the designs to fit.

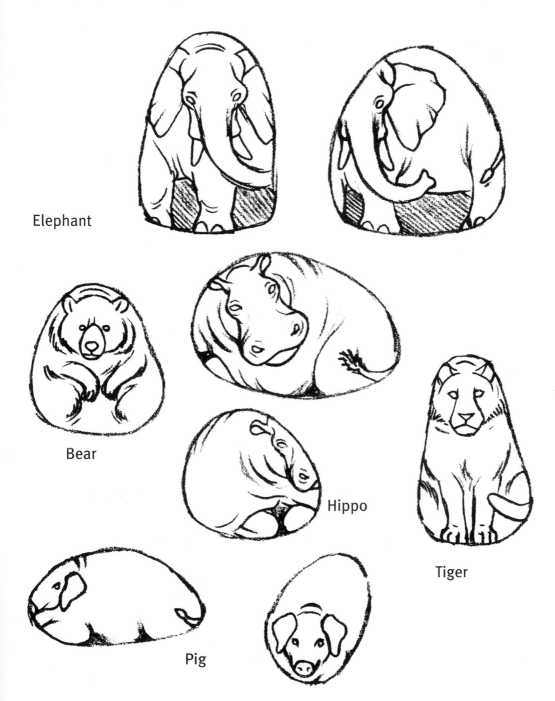

Elephant

Bear

Hippo

Tiger

Pig

COLORFUL CORNUCOPIA: PAINTING REALISTICALLY

Rocks make wonderful vegetables and fruits for a perfect centerpiece on your autumn dining table—it's great fun to match the rocks to vegetable shapes; you will find they're all there, as if Mother Nature had purposefully sculpted them. Painting a rock already shaped like its intended outcome is a wonderful bonus; your job is half done before you start.

Fantasy Harvest This intriguing harvest cornucopia is surprisingly easy to create with a few simple painting techniques. The realistic water droplets create even more interest by adding a "fresh from the field" look.

Step One To duplicate my cornucopia, find rocks with the same general shapes as the ones shown here, starting clockwise from the top left: bell pepper (flat top and distinct pepper shape), corn (smooth and oblong with rounded ends), squash (rough, pockmarked surface and distinct squash shape), onion (round and smooth), apple (flat or indented top, with apple shape), tomato (smooth, oval), carrot (distinct carrot shape with tapered end), and potato (roundish with a few pockmarks and/ or cracks). Of course, you can use other shapes for different vegetables or fruits, but whatever you choose, use photos or real produce for reference.

Step Two For the corn, start by sketching the lines of the husk with a colored pencil. Paint the background of the kernel section with dark brown (burnt umber mixed with a touch of black). Then generously load the round brush with yellow and paint the kernels themselves, one row at a time. There should be enough color on the brush to paint a solid kernel with one short, soft stroke. When the yellow is dry, highlight each kernel with a dot of white.

Step Three Using the flat brush, paint the leaves with light green (green mixed with a touch of white). This requires two painting sessions—you'll need to let the top dry before turning the rock over to paint the underside. Drybrush soft strokes of a slightly darker green (add a touch of black) from the top to about halfway down with the round brush. Using a liner or angled brush, follow the curves of the design to paint long, thin vertical lines around the leaves with a thinned, even darker green (add more black). Then add the lines of thinned white.

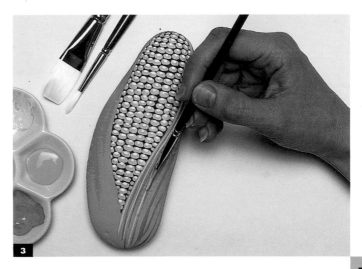

55

Step Four For the squash, choose a pockmarked rock. Paint it with at least two coats of yellow using the flat brush and let it dry. Apply dark green (green with touches of burnt umber and phthalo blue) markings with wide, uneven lines that taper toward the top, wiggling and turning the brush as you drag it upward, leaving a small yellow circle at the top. Paint additional shorter lines at the bottom where the natural markings are denser, and add occasional small strokes between the lines on the rest of the body. Sketch the stem with a black colored pencil—the bottom edge is scalloped, and the top edge is rounded. Paint the stem sides dark green and the top white; then stipple a muted green on the center of the top. Next use black to add vertical lines around the sides and to outline the scalloped edge.

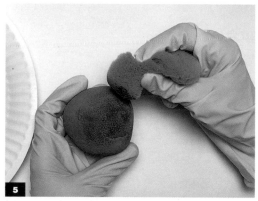

Step Five For the potato, use a fine-grain sponge and apply beige (white with a touch of burnt umber), one side at a time. (I recommend wearing rubber gloves to protect your hands.) After the base color is dry, dip a course-grain sponge in burnt umber mixed with a bit of black, and dab it on a piece of paper to remove the excess. Squeeze the sponge in your fingers, and lightly dab the brown randomly. Try not to overdo this technique, or you'll lose the textured effect. With the round brush, accentuate the cracks and pockmarks with light dabs of dark burnt umber.

Step Six Because orange is very transparent, paint a white base to begin the carrot. After the base has dried, use the gradation technique described on page 7 to paint around the top of the carrot with light green, white, and orange. Use long strokes as you turn the rock for a smooth, uninterrupted blend. Keep turning and softly stroking until you are satisfied. Prop the carrot up on folded paper while it dries so the paint doesn't touch your work surface.

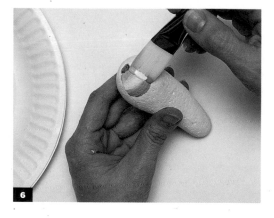

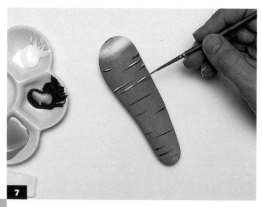

Step Seven Paint the orange base with the flat brush, feathering into the orange of the gradation, and then let it dry. Using red, paint short, random creases with a liner brush. Then highlight the creases with thinned white. Keep your strokes light and quick, always moving in the same direction, touching down and then gently lifting off. Paint the stem at the top with dark green or black, and stipple the edge with white. (The apple is done the same way as the carrot, using red instead of orange and omitting the creases. If you want to add a stem and a leaf to the top of your apple, remember to paint a shadow under the leaf for dimension, as in steps 12 and 13.)

Step Eight Paint the entire onion a light golden beige (mix beige, white, yellow, and orange) with the flat brush, one side at a time. When you are done with the base, cover your mixture with plastic wrap, and save it for the next step. (See "Preserving Your Mixed Colors" on page 32.) Paint the root area using burnt umber with a touch of black . With the round or liner brush, stipple the edge with white. Then paint white, wiggly lines in the hole for the roots.

Step Nine Add a little red and orange to your base mixture to get a rosier beige. With the round brush, use soft, dry vertical strokes all around the onion, radiating from the root area to the opposite side. Do not paint all the way up to the root; leave about 1/4" open. Then use a liner or angled brush to add thin, white vertical lines from the root to the opposite side. Keep your strokes very light and long, moving your whole arm as you paint.

Step Ten For the bell pepper, first sketch the crown on the top of the rock with a colored pencil. Pepper crowns are shaped like polygons, with lines that radiate from the center stem. Paint the base color with the flat brush, and apply two coats if needed. Peppers come in a variety of colors, so experiment with reds, yellows, greens, and oranges. Let it dry. Then use the wet layering technique (see page 7) and the round brush to add a deep shading around the crown's edge.

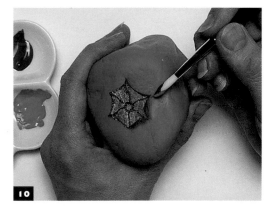

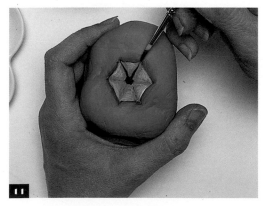

Step Eleven Paint the crown sections medium green with the round brush, letting the sketch lines show through. Apply yellow to the middle, outer edges of each section with dry, feathered strokes. Use black on the round or liner brush to paint the stem, to line the outer crown edges, and to create the radiating lines. Stipple white around the edge and into the center of the stem area. Highlight the points of the pepper's crown by brushing white onto each side of the point and up the radiating line, tapering off quickly.

Step Twelve For the tomato, sketch five or six long, thin leaves with a colored pencil. Paint the rock red (you may need two coats) with the flat brush and allow it to dry. Mix a little black with the red—just enough to make it slightly darker. Use this dark color and dry, feathered strokes to create four or five evenly spaced "dents" that radiate down about a third of the way from the leaves.

Step Thirteen Next add black or dark green to your dark red mixture. Stroke the brush on paper to blot off excess paint. Then brush shadows under the leaves using light, feathered strokes, gradually building the color. Consider your light source before you begin, and keep the shadows thinner than the widths of the leaves. Paint the tomato leaves a medium green. Then use black for the stem and for the short tapered lines that radiate from it. Using a liner brush, highlight the outer edges of the leaves with light green. You don't have to cover every edge, but do highlight over the shadows. Then add spots of white over the light green leaves that are highest. I added a few water droplets to make the tomato look even fresher. (See the box below and the finished project on page 54.) After the paint is dry, assemble your own colorful cornucopia!

WATER DROPLETS

To create realistic-looking water droplets, use the flat brush. Beginning with the bottom portion of the droplet, double-load the brush in red (or whatever color was used on the base) and white. Placing the white at the bottom of the brush, make a C stroke down the left side, around the bottom, and up the right side. Repeat this process for the top of the droplet, using red and a contrasting darker red. Place the darker red at the top, and begin on the left side; then make a C stroke up, around the top, and down the right side. Next mix a bit more dark green or black with the darker red for the shadow color. Using the round brush, paint a shadow under the droplet with dry, feathered strokes. Finish with white highlights in the upper portion where the paint is dark.

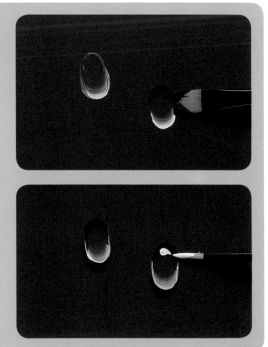

"PURR-FECTLY" ADORABLE DOORSTOP: BUILDING STRUCTURE

Cats have a permanent place in the hearts of many humans, and a painted kitty is a welcome addition to any cat lover's home. Rock cats work perfectly as a doorstop; or you can simply decorate a corner of your home with this lifelike creation. These hand-painted pets require no feeding, and make wonderful gifts to feline fans. Try painting rock pet portraits too!

Designer Doorstop Rocks don't generally sport convenient nubs for ears, so this project demonstrates how to build them using wood filler. You can also use the wood filler to make a flat base for your doorstop.

Step One Use a roughly cylindrical rock that is slightly smaller at the top. Begin by drawing your design on the rock with colored pencil. (See the cat template on page 63.) Adjust the template to fit your rock: An uneven surface can be placed at the back or a bump on the front can become a lifted paw. If your rock does not have a flat base, you can build one with wood filler and let it harden before starting. Next decide where the ears will go; they will be built in two steps to prevent the filler from sagging. Begin with a thin cone of wood filler, molded to almost the intended height of the ear. Be patient—it can be a little sticky, so use a light touch for molding. When the cones are hard, apply more wood filler over them to mold the final ear shapes. Follow the manufacturer's recommended drying time before starting to paint.

Step Two When the wood filler is dry, sketch the insides of the ear. Paint the base colors, leaving enough of the pencil lines unpainted to still see the design. The flat brush works well and achieves good coverage, but you may also use the round brush for smaller areas, such as the muzzle and ears. Cover the body with medium gray (black mixed with white), and paint the insides of the ears pink. Add more white to the gray mix to make it lighter and use this color for the muzzle. Leave the eyes and the nose unpainted.

Step Three Using black, define the design by outlining the ears, eyes, nose, and muzzle with a liner brush. Switch to the round brush and drybrush the shadows on the edges and centers of the ears with feathered strokes. Define the body contours: the neck, legs, toes, haunches, and tail. Then fill in the shadowed areas: between the front legs and between the front legs and the haunches. Paint the body markings using light strokes in the direction the fur would naturally lie.

Step Four Use a liner brush to paint the body fur a light gray. Use individual strokes and paint in the direction the fur would grow. On the face, the fur radiates out from the nose; on the haunches, the fur follows their curves. Paint some hairs lightly over the black body markings, and paint hairs into the black shadow areas to create a furry look. Leave dark areas on the tops of the paws, the bridge of the nose, and under the eyes.

Step Five Paint the long, soft hairs in the ears with white. Also use white to highlight the following areas: the fur below the ears and around the face, the chest spots, the edges of the haunches, the paws, the front legs above the paws, and the tail. Add details to finish the eyes and nose. (See the box below.) Then carefully paint the white hairs around the eyes. Add white fur to the muzzle, concentrating on the nose and the middle of the chin. Finally paint three or four rows of dots on the muzzle with black, and paint the long curving whiskers with white.

5

DETAILING THE EYES AND NOSE

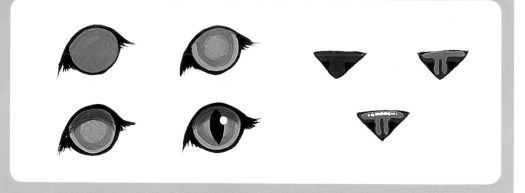

Eyes First paint the irises green. (Or use yellow-brown for topaz eyes.) Add some white and yellow to the green, and highlight the perimeter of each iris, excluding the portion just below the upper lid. Then use the same color to highlight the center. Next mix black with green, and paint a shadow beneath the upper lid using soft strokes. Finally paint the pupil, and add a white dot that overlaps the iris.

Nose Add a touch of black to pink for a magenta base color. Lighten the magenta with white, and highlight the nose (leaving a magenta line on the bottom portion). Carefully stipple a white highlight across the top.

CAT TEMPLATES

Front

Back

ROCK PAINTING THE YEAR 'ROUND

Rock painting possibilities are endless, as is the supply of interesting and exciting rocks to paint. Your artistic eye will develop quickly once you have begun to transform three-dimensional natural stones into vividly colored and unique works of art.

Make rock painting a special part of your holidays, and paint your own dazzling decorations. You can even involve your family and create new holiday traditions. Instead of decorating real eggs (which almost never get eaten!) with dyes, you can create permanent hand-painted Easter eggs to hide and display. Children will love painting spooky eyeballs and ghosts for Halloween. And a beautifully detailed Nativity scene makes a wonderful Christmas gift.

Since nature provides the canvas and the inspiration, rock painting never fails to spark the imagination. Revel in this fascinating venue for artistic expression, and enjoy your new rock painting adventures!